USHER

The godson of soul

SIMON SPOTLIGHT
An imprint of Simon & Schuster
Children's Publishing Division
1230 Avenue of the Americas
New York, New York 10020

Text copyright © 2005 by Chris Nickson
All rights reserved, including the right of reproduction in
whole or in part in any form.
SIMON SPOTLIGHT and colophon are registered
trademarks of Simon & Schuster, Inc.
Manufactured in the United States of America
First Edition
2 4 6 8 10 9 7 5 3 1
ISBN-13: 978-1-4169-0922-4
ISBN-10: 1-4169-0922-2

Library of Congress Catalog Card Number 2005924767

USHER

The godson of soul

by chris nickson

Simon Spotlight

New York   London   Toronto   Sydney

introduction

From the moment he released his first disc in 1994, Usher Raymond IV, known to everyone as Usher, has been building his momentum like a machine. By the time he put out 1997's *My Way* (which he recorded just after graduating high school!) with its smash hit single, "You Make Me Wanna . . . ," he had achieved critical mass. That single was just the first of his number-one hits, and the album was just the beginning in a slew of albums that would push the creative envelope and reach unbelievable heights!

But that was simply the beginning. A couple of years later he put out *Usher Live*, and began a movie career that saw him in no less than three major studio features in the space of a year. By 2001 Usher was back on top of the charts with "U Remind Me," an immediate number one from his stunning, four-times-platinum album *8701*. He had a tight grip on America's pop charts and couldn't set a foot wrong. The following February, Usher won his first GRAMMY Award, Best Male R&B Vocal Performance, for "U Remind Me." Then he helped out P. Diddy—who'd helped produce Usher's debut album—on "I Need a Girl (Part One)." By May 2002, "I Need A Girl (Part One)" hit the top ten, and by the end of the year Usher had stacked an entire shelf full of awards—BET's award for Best Male R&B Artist, and no less than three from *Billboard* to name a few. VH1 had named him one of its "100 Sexiest Artists," and he'd delivered his first concert DVD, *Live Evolution 8701*. Usher had arrived in fine style, and he was only twenty-four.

How could he top that? Easily, it seemed. In 2003 he added a second GRAMMY to his collection, this time for Best Male R&B Vocal Performance for "U Don't Have to Call," and went back into the studio to cut some serious tunes. He was growing quickly as a singer and an artist, yet he hadn't even come close to reaching the top of his game. He was certainly getting there, though, and through long months of hard work, he pushed himself to create an album that would show the world that *he* was the driving force for creativity in contemporary R&B. On this task he commented in an interview with insidecx.com, "It's a challenge for me. I want to make legendary music, not music just for the times. You have to give life a chance to show you what's real. . . . That's why I take my time making albums."

The first fruits of all that labor appeared in January 2004 when "Yeah!" hit the Top 40. With help from fellow Atlantan Ludacris and the master of crunk Lil Jon, the irresistible single sizzled higher and higher and became almost a fixture in the number-one spot, spending a total of twelve weeks there! As Usher explains on his official Web site, usherworld.com, "The mission in my career before now was to 'get' to the party! Now I feel I'm 'at' the party!"

But it had already gone far beyond that; Usher *was* the party. And he was just getting started. When his new album, *Confessions*, arrived in March, it broke all records, selling a staggering 1.1 million copies in its first week; no male R&B artist had ever accomplished such a feat! By July he hit it big with another record, becoming the third artist in history to have *three* singles in the top ten at the same time. "Burn" had the top slot, where it remained for two weeks.

The everlasting "Yeah!" was still hanging on top at number two, while "Confessions Part II" crashed in at number eight. Usher was officially in the company of music's greatest artists; having three hits in the top ten was a feat only managed by the Beatles and the BeeGees, and one that hadn't been achieved for over 20 years.

To celebrate this amazing accomplishment, Usher spent most of 2004 in the spotlight and out on the town. After splitting with his girlfriend of three years, Rozonda "Chilli" Thomas of TLC, Usher was spotted partying all over town with celebrities, pop stars, and even supermodels, including the glamorous Naomi Campbell, although their connection seemed to come to a swift end. He also spent a good portion of 2004 on the road with his sell-out Truth Tour, which began in August and kept him traveling for the remainder of the year.

Despite his busy touring schedule, he just couldn't stay away from the charts. "My

Boo," a duet with chanteuse Alicia Keys, stormed the top ten. This duet track was included on a new version of *Confessions* that hit the shelves in September 2004, as the original album went seven-times platinum. As the year closed, he collaborated with Lil Jon and Ludacris on the crunk-driven "Lovers and Friends," as he watched his own "Caught Up" move into the Top 40.

He was the King, and there was no doubt about it. In fact, at the end of the year, the music trade magazine *Billboard* called him exactly that, the King. Not only was he the king of the charts, lasting seven whole months in the number one position, but he was the king of the award circuit as well. Usher ended 2004 with four Teen Choice Awards, followed by a pair of MTV Video Music Awards about a month later. Just four weeks after that he strolled home with three World Music Awards, and by the end of November, he'd picked up two MTV Europe Awards, followed by a staggering eleven Billboard Music Awards.

His luck didn't end with the calendar, however, and Usher kicked off the new year in January with a People's Choice Award for Favorite Male Singer and a remarkable eight GRAMMY nominations. From his voice that can ignite millions of hearts to his smiling face and six-pack abs, Usher has amassed millions of fans from around the world and astounding recognition from music's favorite icons. He's talented, and he's ambitious, and he's not about to sit back on his laurels. "Down time is not the name of the game," he told insidecx.com in an interview, and he has no intentions of slowing down. In fact, he has plans to branch out with his talents, starring in a major motion picture that is due out later in 2005, reportedly playing an R&B singer—a role that was written for him.

Right now Usher's career seems to be at its peak, but who knows what the future will bring for this bright, young star. With three more well-deserved GRAMMYs on his trophy shelf and a primetime nod from the godfather of soul himself, James Brown, this might just be another beginning for the king of pop and newly crowned "god-son of soul."

chapter one

some people come out of the crib singing and never stop. Others come to it a bit later. For Usher Raymond IV, the love of singing took about nine years to brew, but once it clicked inside of him, there was no turning back.

Usher was born on October 14, 1978, in Chattanooga, Tennessee. His parents divorced when he was young, and he spent his adolescent years with his mom and his younger brother, James. Chattanooga was situated in southern Tennessee, close to the Georgia border and one of Tennessee's greatest tourist attractions, the Smoky Mountains, and home to just over 150,000 people. His mom, Jonnetta Patton, was a hard-working, single mom, and a woman who'd attended a Baptist church all her life. She loved music, and was a good singer herself, so when the chance to become the choir director at St. Elmo's Missionary Baptist Church in town presented itself in 1987, she jumped at the job.

Music had always been present in Usher's life, on the radio, on the television, in church, but it had never really hit him. He went to school, played with his friends, and went to church. He had typical boyish aspirations of becoming a football or basketball star, but he wasn't really serious about them. He sang a little around the house, enough for his mother to know he had a good voice, although it wasn't a talent he particularly wanted to pursue at first. In fact, when Jonnetta took the position as choir director, she almost had to force him to join. At the time Usher was nine years old, and his brother was a toddler. Having the two boys join the choir meant that she didn't have to find a babysitter for them while she was at practices, and it would enable her to keep a closer eye on both her sons. To her surprise, and even more to his, Usher discovered (once he'd given in to the idea) that he loved opening his mouth and hearing wonderful music come out. The hymns were moving, and the sound of the massed voices singing together stirred him in a way he'd never imagined possible. Singing touched him, and soon he couldn't get enough of it; it became his passion in life, replacing sports, replacing everything.

Although singing became a passion, he never thought it was something he could actually do for a living until his aunt took him to see New Edition in concert when they played in

Chattanooga. They were, in many ways, the first boy band, still teenagers when they'd started out in 1982. From 1985 through the early 1990s, New Edition scored a string of hits and jump-started the careers of members Bobby Brown and Johnny Gill, as well as the group Bell Biv DeVoe (who in turn mentored '90s R&B sensation Boyz II Men). Seeing New Edition perform was a life-changing experience for Usher. Reminiscing about the concert, he told *The Dallas Morning News*, "I remember the choreography, I remember the lights, I remember the crowd screaming, the lights, the excitement . . . I had a horrible seat, but that was one of the highlights of my life, man. It was one of the things that made me want to do this."

He was barely ten years old and still new to singing, but possessed a remarkable voice that stood out even in a good choir. And after realizing that it was possible to make a career out of his passion, he knew what he wanted to do with his life—he wanted to be a singer. Michael Jackson had come into his superstardom with *Thriller*. His epic, groundbreaking videos and dance moves were all over television. Prince had hit it big with *Purple Rain*. It was a new golden age for African-American artists, and there were plenty of role models for a young performer to aspire to.

Local music entrepreneur Darryl Wheeler had been eyeballing the success of New Edition, and in 1990, sensing the endless possibilities for success, he decided to start a similar band. He held auditions and had soon recruited five members—Anthony Byrd, Adrian Johnson, Charles Yarborough, Reginald McKibbens ... and Usher Raymond IV. These five boys became Nu Beginning. After some rehearsals and a few shows around Chattanooga, Wheeler took the quintet into the studio, where they recorded the album *Nu Beginning*. Recording an album was the highlight of Usher's young life. He had visions of being discovered, of the group's hits immediately storming the charts and their videos appearing on MTV. He was young, and he could dream. Unfortunately, at the ages of ten, eleven, and twelve respectively, there was no way these young boys could have been taken seriously enough to attract any real attention from the music industry, no matter how talented they were. In the music business, Chattanooga was considered a back-water. Nu Beginning never really had a chance at making Usher's lofty dreams come true. Usher might have decided to dedicate his life to music, but the other members weren't as passionate about it. Their interests shifted, especially as girls began to enter the picture.

After Nu Beginning disbanded, Usher went back to singing in the church choir and living life as a regular twelve-year-old boy. Although his interest in singing didn't waver, Usher shared the other boys' interest in girls. Usher was in no way immune to their charms; however, it might come as a shock that not all the girls he fancied fell for him. One day he was hanging out at the ice-skating rink, and he saw a girl with whom he wanted to skate. Naturally he decided that the best way to go about accomplishing this was by grabbing her arm. She instantly pulled away and refused to skate with him. His mother witnessed the whole encounter, as Usher later recalled in an interview with *Teen People Magazine*, "My mother watched the whole thing, and when we got into the parking lot, she whipped my butt. She told me, 'never touch a woman like that. If I catch you doing it again, I promise to break your arm off!' That left a lasting impression."

Apparently his mother's threat couldn't keep Usher away from the ladies, and later on in his twelfth year, Usher experienced his first real kiss at Dalewood Middle School. It was just before first period, and he was on his way to class with his best friend. Usher asked Erica, a girl both he and his friend knew, if she'd kiss them. And she did. Like singing, the experience was a life-changing moment in his young life, and he was so swept up in that moment he was late to class!

However much he enjoyed girls, singing remained his primary focus. He learned a great deal in church about how to project his voice and how to emote when he sang. The tunes and style of the church hymns gave his voice a rare quality that not many pop stars have. So many of the soul and R&B greats had gotten their start singing in the gospel church choirs on Sundays. Soul and R&B music had been honored and respected in African-American culture for decades, and even though Usher didn't realize it yet, he was following in the footsteps of legendary African-American musicians, a lineage that included the great Sam Cooke, Al Green, and far beyond.

By the time Usher turned thirteen, it was obvious to Jonnetta that his passion for music wasn't going to go the way of all his previous boyish ambitions. It was here to stay, and not only was this interest unwavering, but he was actually working at it. He'd developed into a singer of real talent and promise. With time, training, and guidance, his dream could become reality. Although she knew well enough that the odds of him ever becoming a big star were slim, she stood behind him and his seemingly unreachable dream. One thing was for sure, though: It wasn't going to happen in Chattanooga. It might be a place singers came from, but it wasn't where they were discovered. For a long time, producers of mainstream music had centered themselves in either New York or Los Angeles. In the '60s a place much closer to Usher's home—Memphis—had been the home of soul powerhouse Stax Records, and in the late 1980s, another city popped up on the map, even closer than Memphis, where Usher might be able to try his luck.

Kenneth "Babyface" Edmonds and Antonio "L.A." Reid had enjoyed plenty of hits as part of soul/funk band the Deele. From there they'd moved into production and writing, scoring hits with artists like the Whispers and Pebbles. Babyface had started performing solo, and his *Tender Lover* had been a smash, spawning no less than four hit R&B singles. In 1989 the duo moved to Atlanta and formed LaFace Records, which had a deal with the major recording label Arista. Rather than gathering a slew of so-so singers, Edmonds and Reid took their time searching for a local talent who would be good enough to go national, and they had a canny touch. Their first artist, Toni Braxton, became an immediate sensation in 1991 with her hit "Love Shoulda Brought You Home." LaFace Records followed that up with hits by Jermaine Jackson (brother of Michael), and a trio of Atlanta-born female singers, TLC.

LaFace wasn't the only game in town, however. Young producer Jermaine Dupri had been making waves too. At the age of fourteen he produced a hit for Silk Tymes Leather, and two years later had his own production company, So So Def. In 1991 he spotted a pair of young hip-hoppers playing at an Atlanta mall and took them into the recording studio. They emerged as Kris Kross, and produced "Jump," a single that soared to the top of the charts. Dupri then signed another big group, Xscape. Atlanta was turning into Hotlanta. The city itself had grown; it shook off its sleepy, southern image and reinvented itself as a bustling, cosmopolitan hub. For an aspiring singer, it was the new land of opportunity. And it was just a couple of hours away from Chattanooga.

To thirteen-year-old Usher, though, a hundred miles might as well have been a million. He couldn't take a bus down there by himself, and his mother didn't have the luxury to leave work and shuttle him back and forth. It was so close, but still so far away. What he didn't know was that his mother was also thinking about Atlanta and its possibilities. She knew what was happening there musically (and if she hadn't, her son would have readily informed her), and she understood how good it could be for Usher's career. "I saw the hard work, I saw the dedication," she told *Sister 2 Sister* magazine. "I saw that drive that he had to be successful. I saw the superstardom in him from the beginning." She believed in her son; she desperately wanted him to fulfill his dream. Although she had a life, a home, and a good job in Chattanooga, she understood her son's driving ambition and vowed to find a way to make it happen, no matter what she had to give up. Atlanta wasn't too far away, and she knew that her family network would be close by if she needed them.

Usher was still overwhelmed when his mother told him they were all moving to Atlanta. It was almost too much to take in. His life was about to be turned upside down. Leaving the place they had called home for years was difficult for everyone. Usher had a steady girlfriend in Chattanooga, his first serious relationship. Once he found out he was leaving he had no choice but to break up with her. Long-distance phone calls were not an option, and he didn't want to be pen pals. "The situation broke my heart," he recalled later to *Teen People Magazine*. "She kissed me and we said good-bye. And nobody ever knew it—but I cried and cried." It was a sacrifice, but every artist has to make choices for his career. That one, though, the very first, felt like the hardest.

Atlanta was a new experience for the whole family. For Jonnetta it was a new job; for Usher and his brother, James, it was a new school. And for all of them it was a brand-new neighborhood with new kids and new rules. It was disorienting, and it took a while before they were used to their new city; after all, it was much bigger than Chattanooga, a real cosmopolitan hub. But Usher didn't forget why they'd moved. He practiced hard and he learned all that he could. He was focused on what he wanted, and they hadn't been in Atlanta too long before he saw what might be his big break.

Star Search, the syndicated television talent show, was coming to town. They were open to new performers, and it would be a great introduction to the stage for Usher. Of course, he'd sung in church before, both as part of the choir and as a soloist, so he was used to an audience. This, though, would be a real proving ground for him. Jonnetta took him early to the auditions, and he waited eagerly and nervously for his chance. At fourteen years old, his voice was just beginning to develop the silky quality that would later come to the foreground and mark him as something special. This was his big moment, the thing he'd been waiting for since he was nine. He stood up before the critical audience and sang his heart out, putting every ounce of emotion into the notes, just the way his mother had taught him. When he finished, there was a stunned silence. His heart was beating quickly as he tried to figure out whether they loved him or hated him. Then the waves of applause came crashing, and a smile filled his face. When the votes were counted, he'd won the teen section. He couldn't believe it at first. He'd won! His mother hugged him, and suddenly the world had become a much bigger place. He really could do this!

He'd barely recovered from the thrill of winning, still clutching his mom to be sure everything was real, when a man came up to them and blew his world apart. He told them that he worked in A&R (artist and repertoire) for LaFace Records, and that he wanted Usher to come down to the studio. This was *it*. This was what he'd dreamed about almost every day for the last five years, the thing that had filled his thoughts. And now it was almost a reality. There was one hurdle left, and it was the biggest of them all, auditioning for L.A. Reid, the head of the label.

chapter two

It was impossible for Usher not to be nervous as his mother drove him to the label's plush office. Everything depended on this; he felt as if his entire future rested on this moment, and perhaps it really did.

As a musician himself, Reid knew the boy would be nervous, and tried to put him at ease, giving him the chance to relax before asking him to sing. Finally, though, it could be put off no longer, and Usher opened his mouth and sang. The sounds that came out were filled with confidence, attitude, and a level of maturity that was far beyond his years. Contactmusic.com reported that Reid said he knew right away that Usher would be a star, commenting "there was a look in [Usher's] eyes when I met him at thirteen years old, and that look said if you intend to associate yourself with the next major super-star, you'd better associate yourself with me." Reid knew immediately that the young, skinny kid before him had exactly what it took to become a big, big star. He was still raw, and it was going to take a lot of work, but the material was there to be molded.

Although Reid wanted to sign Usher right away, there were still details to be arranged. Nothing was as simple as a signa-ture on the dotted line. Jonnetta had to hire a lawyer to represent her son, and meet with the label's lawyer. Taking on a minor meant a lot of responsibility. And, of course, Usher couldn't legally make his own deci-sions; Jonnetta made all the decisions, always keeping her son's best interests at heart. To make sure that no one took advantage of him, she became his manager. Usher always appreciated his mother's help, and trusted her to do the right thing. As he told teenmusic.com, "My mother is a true go-getter . . . She saw that I had talent and she had to make many sacrifices to make it happen. I'm very grateful. She does an amazing job. . . . There is a very thin line between balancing a personal life and business but I think she does a great job at balancing the two." Finally, after what seemed like forever, the deal was made. Usher was bursting to get into the studio and begin what he knew would be his real future.

The first thing L.A. Reid wanted to do was get Usher used to working in the studio. So as not to intimidate him from the start, Reid didn't set Usher up with any big names at first. Instead he set Usher up with a local group of producers, whom Reid had come to know, called Organized Noize.

Organized Noize was comprised of Rico Wade, Pat "Sleepy" Brown, and Ray Murray. They aimed to be the Atlanta equivalent of Dr. Dre and the Bomb Squad. They didn't sing, they made and programmed beats. Their studio, which they called the Dungeon, was the basement of Wade's mother's house. As its name suggests, their studio was neither inspiring nor high tech. The room was unfinished. There was a Georgia, red-clay floor, and the only available seating was on the steps or a couple of beat-up lawn chairs. Their equipment was all secondhand, and it broke down on more than one occasion.

The Organized Noize crew had other artists they worked with, like a young OutKast, and they had just finished a TLC remix for LaFace Records, but helping Usher create a few complete tracks was a big paying job for them. At the time, Wade was still working in a beauty supply store to make ends meet, so they put in the time and the effort, and within a few months they presented finished masters to Reid.

He liked what he heard. Usher could really cut it in the studio, unlike many aspiring singers. He still sounded young, but that was inevitable. Reid took one of the tracks, "Call Me a Mack," and made a deal for it to be on the soundtrack of the upcoming movie, *Poetic Justice*. In 1993 "Call Me a Mack" became Usher's recording debut, although, to this day, few of his fans know about the cut. "I hate that they did forget about it," Usher would tell the online publication, *LAUNCH*, a few years later, "but it was a really great record. It says a lot about me . . . where I come from and what I've evolved to." The world hardly noticed it at the time, but for Usher and his mother this recording was a defining moment in his career, and in both of their lives. He'd made it, and opened the door to bigger things. And L.A. Reid thought so too. The trial run was over. Usher had proven that he could harness his talent; it was time to start work on his first album.

Making an album is a full-time job, and for a fourteen-year-old that presented a problem. He wouldn't be able to go to school full-time, get all his homework done, and work in the studio at the same time, especially since Reid decided to send him to New York to record. Instead, it was arranged for him to have a tutor in the Big Apple.

Reid made Usher's first album into a big-budget affair, involving a number of high-profile producers such as Al B. Sure and Puff Daddy (currently known as P. Diddy). On the heels of the popularity of New Jack Swing, R&B was coming into its own, and a generation of young artists, including Tevin Campbell, Mary J. Blige, and R. Kelly, was starting to emerge on the scene. Reid believed Usher could establish himself at the head of that pack if he had the right production and the right songs. Reid felt it was worth spending the money to make Usher into a star, and one who would shine brightly for years to come. To Reid, this wasn't spending; it was an investment.

And for Usher it was the adventure of a lifetime. Not only was he going to record his own album, but he'd be doing it in New York, a place he'd never seen before. Contrary to what he'd imagined, Usher did not get to experience the glamour and glitz of the big stars in the Big Apple. He spent his days and evenings working in the studio, or with his tutor catching up on his schoolwork. He fell asleep at night exhausted, only to wake up to start the same routine again the next day. But it *was* exhilarating. This was what he'd wanted to do with his life, and it was happening. He didn't mind working on take after take of a vocal with a demanding producer or listening to endless discussions over the playback of a track. With every single minute he was learning new things and improving himself as an artist. He loved building a track, and then finishing the vocals and backing vocals and hearing the song come together. He was determined to be the best, and he was absorbing it all like a sponge.

Reid spared no expense and left no stone unturned in his efforts to make this album, and with the major production and writing talents employed behind the young singer, Usher's first album more than lived up to everyone's expectations. "Whispers" was a dark, smooth masterpiece, "Love Was Here" was a celebration of soul, and the easy, midtempo beat of "The Many Ways" became a classic Al B. Sure production. Puff Daddy brought his sampling talent to the party, building grooves around a couple of old tracks—James Brown's "Blind Man Can See It," and "Tidal Wave" from Ronnie Laws.

When the sessions were finally done, and the album was mixed, Usher went back to Atlanta. From that point on, he truly believed it was just a matter of time before he became a star. It seemed to come so easily, as if it was *meant* to happen. L.A. Reid loved the disc, and thought it was a perfect slice of R&B for the market. He especially loved Donnell Jones's composition, "Think of You," with its synth-heavy hook and beat. That, he decided, would be Usher's first single.

The album, *Usher*, arrived in stores on August 30, 1994. By then, his single "Think of You" was already receiving plenty of airplay and starting to rise on the R&B charts. Everything was going according to plan. The reviews were good, and the single continued to climb. Soon the single was in the top ten of the R&B charts. Usher had scored a hit with his very first record! Of course he was proud of it, anyone would be. It was a major moment in his life, the success that every artist hopes for, confirming what he already knew to be true, that this was what he was meant to do.

There was only one problem. "Think of You" was doing well, but the album wasn't selling, and no one, least of all Usher, understood why at the time. In retrospect, critics have said that *Usher* was a great R&B record—but that's all it was. However, at that time, the R&B albums that were doing big sales had all crossed over from classic R&B into the mainstream pop genre. Their tracks played on MTV and Top 40 radio. It is true that *Usher* was soulful, smooth, and full of talent, but there was nothing mainstream about it.

It wasn't his fault. He'd recorded the songs everyone wanted him to sing and done an incredible job. His star talent was obvious, and his voice was riveting and beautiful to listen to, but his record just didn't have what it took to break out in that musical climate.

As the first building block in a career, it was nothing less than wonderful, the kind of a record an artist ten years older than

Usher would be proud to call his own. But the bottom line was that his debut was not a commercial success. Once it became apparent that it wasn't going to be a hit, a few people he'd worked with didn't even want to know him anymore. A couple of fellow artists were suddenly too busy to take or return his calls. Usher was proud of the work he'd done, but now he was made to feel as though perhaps he should not have been. He felt alone, and unsure of what was going to happen next.

Then the inevitable happened: His voice finally broke. When he hit puberty, he lost his voice completely. For a singer, losing your voice is not only the end of a passion, but also the end of one's livelihood. He had to work with the best vocal coaches in Atlanta to get back his voice, which had altered significantly since it had broken, and there was much he had to relearn. It was, perhaps, the biggest hurdle he'd had to overcome on his way to his massive success.

That he was able to do it at all was a testament to his determination to make it to the top.

In an interview with the online publication, *LAUNCH*, he recalled, "My biggest heartbreak I felt was being abandoned. A lot of the lessons you learn later on in life, I learned at an early age. When I was fifteen, I knew what it was to be a man. If you don't have a successful record, people start to doubt you. At one point in time I felt like didn't nobody care about me. I had lost my voice, and was at my lowest point."

But there were two people who still believed in him, and helped him regain confidence in himself. His mother was always there, offering her unconditional love and support. She knew he was talented, and that ultimately he'd bounce back from this setback a stronger and more capable artist. And L.A. Reid thought so too. He also had unswerving faith that Usher was going to make it, but he decided to ease up on the pressure and allow Usher to live a normal life again for a while.

Usher was going through an awkward adolescence, growing quickly and becoming lanky rather than lithe, and suffering from minor acne, which left him very self-conscious about his appearance. Reid knew, however, that once Usher got past this phase, he'd feel better about himself and he'd be mature enough to go back into the studio and make the smash hit that was simmering inside him. Usher needed the space he was given. He had to find himself, to adjust to the young man he was becoming, and learn to overcome the disappointment that accompanied *Usher.* Despite the loneliness and hurt that he felt from being deserted by some people, the two people who really mattered remained right by his side every step of the way.

Though he was taking a little break, Usher didn't stay completely out of the public eye. He appeared on *Oprah,* where his unaffected, easygoing demeanor charmed an audience of millions, and in 1995 he appeared on the American Music Awards as part of Black Men United, singing "U Will Know," which appeared on the soundtrack to the movie *Jason's Lyric*. He did a gig singing on a Coca-Cola Christmas advertisement, a duet with Monica on her debut album, *Miss Thang*, and last, but not least, a track on *Rhythm of the Games: 1996 Olympic Games Album*. The choice to include a track on this disc was a no-brainer, given that the games were held in Atlanta, and also because it gave people around the globe the chance to hear Usher crooning the song "Dreamin.'" Those few appearances kept him just visible enough to keep people from forgetting about him entirely, while still allowing him to escape the pressures of a full-blown career.

The hiatus gave Usher the chance to have a normal adolescence. He was back in school, dating, and socializing. And although *Usher* didn't grab him as much fame in the music industry as he'd hoped it would, it made him a hero among kids his age. He was the kid with the album. He'd met all the celebrities and had his songs played on the radio. So he laid low for a few years, but knew that when the time was right, he'd have his shot at stardom again.

By the time Usher was finishing his senior year of high school, the time had arrived. Reid knew that Usher was ready to buckle down and work in earnest. However, he also knew that he would have to think long and hard about what direction he wanted this next album to go in. His reputation, and Usher's future, depended on the success of his second album. So, instead of bringing in New York producers, Reid decided to use some hometown talent, and Jermaine Dupri seemed the ideal candidate. A proven hit maker, Dupri was young, just a couple of years older than Usher, and had his finger on the pulse of the new generation of hip-hop and R&B music. He could see the potential in Usher, and he was eager to let it soar. Between the three of them, Reid had faith that they would be able to come up with a great new album. He had no idea just how right he would be.

chapter three

As soon as school let out, with his diploma in hand, Usher got to work on his new album. It had been so long since he'd recorded his first album, and he was eager to return to the studio. So, in the summer of 1996, he rolled up his sleeves and sat down with Jermaine Dupri to plan his next move.

Everyone had learned from the mistakes they had made with the debut, and this time the album would be aimed squarely at the crossover market between R&B and pop, while still keeping true to Usher's soulful roots. Usher helped write several of the tracks, along with Dupri, and Babyface, Reid's partner, who was an acclaimed performer and songwriter in his own right. As Usher told MTV, "I wanted to show people that I've grown a lot since my last album, and writing was a part of that process." Unlike so many vocalists, he never oversang. Keeping this from happening was a deliberate strategy on the part of the producers. The focus of the album was on the subject of romance, which meshed perfectly with Usher's smooth voice, and the lyrics he penned were completely autobiographical. "I just took things from my life and wrote about them," he explained to the online publication, *LAUNCH*. "It's all my vision, which is why I named the album *My Way*." The album's title was also a shout out to one of music's great icons, Frank Sinatra, whose big hit "My Way" served as inspiration for the album.

Though Usher had more influence on his second album then he'd had on his first, Usher's vision was filtered through Jermaine Dupri, who worked very closely with the young star. Usher described Dupri's involvement in an interview for the online publication *LAUNCH*, saying, "If I would meet a girl, he would listen to how I kick my game. If I was on the phone, he would sit next to me and hear what I would say. If I invited someone to the studio, he would listen to how I present myself. That had a lot to do with how he came up with the music that fits me." Since the album wasn't due until September 1997, they weren't in any rush. They took their time in the studio to make sure that everything was just right. There'd be no misfires this time around.

As soon as he recorded the track, everyone knew that "You Make Me Wanna . . ." was a natural single, one certain to be a major hit. It played on the radio at the beginning of the summer, and the video, a slew of carefully selected Usher appearances, went straight into heavy rotation. The video showed him singing at the Circle of Sisters Expo in Atlanta, and all over the country at the Bronner Bros. health and beauty conventions, strutting his stuff to a wide audience. By September 1997 the single was in the Top 40 and already topping the R&B singles chart. Usher began a series of "back-to-school" showcases, performing in high schools and Boys and Girls Clubs all around the United States, followed by concerts on college campuses.

Usher also made his acting debut, appearing on three episodes of the hit teen sitcom *Moesha*, starring fellow singer Brandy. Usher played Jeremy, a football player and honor student, and sometimes, even a bit of a jerk. The show played on Usher's talent and popularity by having Jeremy and Moesha go to an Usher concert on their first date. At the end of the episode, Jeremy sweeps Moesha off her feet by showing her a grand romantic gesture: lip-synching "You Make Me Wanna . . ." to prove his love. Guest starring on *Moesha* was wonderful publicity for the album, and for Usher himself, who displayed a great deal of poise and natural acting ability. Certainly he seemed to enjoy himself, and it wouldn't be too long before he would try his luck on the big screen.

For now, though, there was far too much happening in his music career. By November "You Make Me Wanna . . ." had made it to the top ten, and was still enjoying its eleven-week run at the head of the R&B charts. A month later it hit the top spot on the pop charts and spent three weeks there.

The success of *My Way* was the best Christmas present he could have imagined. And it wasn't the only one he would get. The new year had barely arrived before *My Way* was on top of the R&B album charts. "Nice & Slow," the melodic rap that became the disc's second single, was in the pole spot on three different charts, while "You Make Me Wanna . . ." was perched atop the U.K. charts, becoming an international hit and establishing Usher as a world-famous star.

In February of 1998, Usher was nominated for his first GRAMMY Award, for Best Male R&B Vocal Performance for "You Make Me Wanna. . . ." Although he didn't win, the nomination was a great honor, and a nod of admiration and respect to his artistry.

And then the strangest thing happened: *My Way* simply wouldn't stop selling. Once it passed the million mark, going platinum, Usher thought that it couldn't get any better. But it did. The numbers kept on growing and growing, going from two million to three, as he watched in disbelief. And still the figures kept climbing . . . four million, five million, six million, until finally, a staggering seven million copies were sold! It was so far beyond anything he could have imagined.

It wasn't just the fans who were raving about Usher; reviewers were certainly impressed too. Allmusic.com deemed *My Way* as a disc that "fulfilled his potential . . . a strong second effort that showcases Usher at his best." Rollingstone.com described "You Make Me Wanna . . ." as "tiptoe love funk with a spare gangsta air" and called Usher a "one-man Blackstreet" for his fantastic overdubbing abilities.

Little did Usher know that this was just the beginning. From being almost unknown just a year before, suddenly Usher was everywhere. You couldn't turn on MTV without seeing one of his videos, or listen to the radio with hearing his voice. There was also some time for a few small acting gigs, guest-starring on eight episodes of the soap opera *The Bold and the Beautiful*.

Then came the biggest event yet: the honor of touring with Janet Jackson and being the opening act on her Velvet Rope

Tour which began in July. Janet Jackson was an icon. Not only was she a member of the famous Jackson family, and sister to superstar Michael, but she was a superstar in her own right. Janet had pushed the envelope, not only with her music, but with her dancing as well, and scored more hits than most artists could ever hope for.

As Usher would later tell *LAUNCH*, an online publication, "The thrill of kicking it with Janet was hot. . . . She's a definite entertainer, works hard and sweats every night. . . . I learned a lot about how to make an artist look like a star. On the personal side, I got a chance to hug her."

However, just before he hit the road with Janet Jackson, he filmed a relatively small role in *The Faculty*, just to keep his acting career afloat. A horror film from directors Kevin Williamson and Robert Rodriguez, the movie, which was set in an Ohio high school, was a cross between *Body Snatchers* and *The Breakfast Club*, an unusual blend of tastes. Usher's was just a supporting role, that of student Gabe Santora.

Usher was officially in the big time—he was touring with Janet, topping all the charts, and acting on the big screen. "My Way" soared into the top ten and the *Billboard* Hot 100 Singles, where it remained for three weeks. While he was on the road with Janet, he received an MTV Video Music Award nomination for Best R&B Video. Unfortunately, as with the GRAMMY nomination, he did not end up winning.

By the end of 1998 he was a huge star. There hadn't been a week when he wasn't on one of the charts, and *Billboard*, the music magazine that lists all the bestselling discs, paid him an appropriate honor. Not only was he their number seven Singles Artist of the Year, but he was also nominated for three Billboard Music Awards for video. He also topped their year-end chart as Top Pop Artist (singles and albums), Top Pop Artist—

Male (singles and albums), Top Hot 100 Singles Artist, Top Hot 100 Singles Artist— Male, Top R&B Artist (singles and albums), Top R&B Artist—Male (singles and albums), and Top Hot R&B Singles Artist— Male. And he was just twenty years old.

Usher hadn't just made it, he'd climbed to the top of the mountain. He'd established himself as one of the day's major young R&B artists and crossed over into the vital pop market. On top of that, Usher continued to cultivate his blossoming acting career. By this time his film *The Faculty* had come out. Unlike Usher's concerts and music, the film didn't get good reviews when it appeared, and curiously, the soundtrack of the movie didn't feature Usher at all. But that didn't really matter. He was a hot property, and that meant bigger and better things were on the way. He was already set to film another small role, this time in *She's All That*, a teen comedy that was set in high school, starring Freddie

Prinze Jr. and Rachel Leigh Cook. Usher took the part of Ron James, a campus DJ. After multiple minor and supporting roles, his first starring role lay just around the corner, and he believed he was finally ready for it. He was fascinated by the big screen and eager to spread his wings. And of course, his popularity on the charts meant that he'd be a box-office draw at the movie theater too.

The big question was whether he was a good enough actor with enough experience to be able carry a movie. Well, his family at LaFace had faith that he could, which is why they brought him the script for *Light It Up*. The role was big and powerful, and the film script was intense. Babyface was the executive producer, but his wife Tracey also worked on the project. Keeping it in the family ensured that things would go smoothly, but Usher took everything extremely seriously. In a way this role was a way of paying back L.A. Reid, who'd always believed in him, and whom Usher saw as a father figure. Even when that first album hadn't sold well, Reid never lost faith. He pushed Usher toward television, and encouraged his film ambitions because he believed that Usher had the potential. This was a major step for Usher. He was excited to venture into a different aspect of the entertainment field, but he did not take the role lightly.

He was set to play Lester, a student attending an inner city high school. The film was about standing up for what you believe in, and being willing to put yourself on the line. There was strong acting talent involved in the project, including Forest Whitaker, Judd Nelson, and Sara Gilbert. The movie pointed out the flaws in the educational system, particularly the way that inner city children were treated, and more than anything, that was what attracted Usher to the script. He admitted that the story might have been a little "exaggerated," but his big hope, as told to the online publication, *LAUNCH*, was that it would "better the educational system for our kids, the future." While he hadn't attended an inner city school like *Light It Up*'s Lincoln High, he had visited some, and he understood what conditions were like.

He'd done well on his previous films, but this one would be much more demanding in terms of both time and skill. He knew he had a natural acting talent—it had shone through when he was on *Moesha*—but he had also had an acting coach. The character of Lester required a lot of emotion, and Usher had to be able to draw that from within, to create it from nothing.

How did he do it? As the acting coach showed him, he had to think about the good times he'd experienced, and also all the bad, and put them all together. That would be enough to get him to the point where he could cry, which was something he had to do in the film. The filming hours were long and grueling, and more time was spent standing around on the set and waiting than actually filming. When it was time for a scene, Usher had to snap straight into character. That was a tough enough task for a veteran actor, but for a novice it meant a lot of hard work and concentration. But that was what it was all about, the price he had to pay in order to make his mark in film as well as music.

Though *Light It Up* was only fairly well received by the critics, the fans loved it. Many people were astonished by Usher's acting ability, but even more by the power and passion of the story itself. Teen audiences, in particular, found it very moving— and that, after all, was the target audience. It might have been a fantasy of sorts, but the moral behind it was one that many teenagers could relate to, that of taking charge of their own lives and futures and standing up for what they believe in.

The movie didn't transform Usher into a

major movie star; it was not a blockbuster hit. But it did achieve two things: It proved to Usher that he was a good actor, and it reminded him that the climb up the Hollywood ladder would be a slow one. In music he had already become a major star, and he wasn't about to let that slip away.

chapter four

All of usher's touring, acting, and special appearances meant that he hadn't had any time to write new material or get back into the studio. Fans were clamoring for a new record, any new record by Usher, and there wasn't one. So he sat down with L.A. Reid at LaFace and they came up with the next best thing—a live album.

Usher had spent a lot of time on the road with Janet Jackson and learned a great deal from watching her. Though she wasn't the first star he'd opened for (previously he had opened for Puff Daddy and Mary J. Blige on a few of their concert dates), it had been an unforgettable experience for him, as it was the first time he'd been involved with a big tour and its elaborate production. He loved touring with her, and his fans loved watching him live. He also felt sorry for those fans of his who didn't get to see him live. So, Reid and Usher decided to cull together some performances from the tour on one album. Perhaps as a nod to his hometown, Usher chose the tracks from his two performances in Chattanooga, Tennessee. The album was appropriately named, *Usher Live*, and it hit stores in March 1999.

As he pointed out in an interview with *LAUNCH*, the online publication, he wanted to be able to "show the people who didn't have a chance to see the show what they missed." Well, *Usher Live* gave them exactly that. It came out on CD, but also as a VHS concert tape.

The live video showed his listeners something that the fans who'd had the chance to see him onstage already knew—the guy could dance. His moves came naturally, as did his rhythm—not bad for someone who'd never had a dance lesson in his life. And the screaming that can be heard throughout the music made it obvious that plenty of fans were there for him, not the headliner.

His live set was a mixture of the new hits—"You Make Me Wanna . . . ," "My Way," and "Nice & Slow"—and some of his first big songs, including "Roni" and "Every Little Step." They had planned in advance to tape the shows for a live disc, so plenty of guest stars were on hand to help out, everyone from Babyface himself to Lil' Kim, who offered her vocal styles on "Just Like Me." Even Jermaine Dupri came on stage to help Usher get the sound that had made *My Way* such a huge smash.

With a few exceptions, live albums

generally aren't massive sellers. Rather like greatest hits collections, they tend to sum up a phase of an artist's career. There were some people who said Usher shouldn't have released a live disc so early in his career, that he was mostly a studio singer. That was true; he hadn't done a great deal of live performing. But at the same time, that made *Usher Live* all the more valuable. It proved he really could deliver in concert.

There was no way anyone could reasonably expect *Usher Live* to do as well as *My Way* had done—it had gone through the roof and out to the stratosphere. *Usher Live* didn't even hit the platinum mark, but that was all right. It was a way of marking time, of keeping Usher's name out there. Careerwise there were other things to focus on, and the live CD and video were the perfect solution to the in-between-albums problem. Not only did it give the fans exactly what they wanted, but the CD and video allowed him to take a break from the stresses of singing, so that he could get a real start on his movie career.

On top of his movie-star ambitions, he also had to look ahead to his next studio album, even though that was still quite a way in the future. After the massive success of *My Way* there would be a lot to live up to. The idea was to come up with something better. The album would have to show Usher's development as an artist, stay true to his soulful R&B roots (it wasn't for nothing that Usher listed Stevie Wonder, Michael Jackson, the late Donny Hathaway, the Dazz Band, and Bobby Brown among his big influences), and be able to cross over into mainstream pop as successfully, if not more so, than its predecessor had. It required better songs, stronger technique, focused innovation, and a lot of hard work.

All that meant plenty of planning and preproduction work on the record. But since no one was in a rush, Usher did manage to find the time to squeeze in an appearance on the Disney television series, *The Famous Jett Jackson*. It kept him visible to the public and gave him a chance to flex his acting muscles. Having a guest star of Usher's caliber also gave the series a boost.

On top of the time he spent recording in the studio, he also found time to take part in two more movies. The first was the made-for-television movie, *Geppetto*, which was a comedy based on the Pinocchio story, starring comedians Drew Carey and Julia Louis-Dreyfus, who were both at the height of their popularity.

The second film was quite different. Set in Texas in 1875, *Texas Rangers* was a Western, pure and simple, the tale of several young men (for the most part, then barely known actors James Van Der Beek and Ashton Kutcher, and country music star Randy Travis) trying to keep law and order in the Lone Star State. Usher played Randolph Douglas Scipio, the scout for the troop. It certainly wasn't as large a role as Lester in *Light It Up*, but he did have plenty of screen time.

Despite its handsome young stars, the movie wasn't a box office success. But by the time it appeared, it was already ancient history for Usher. He was back in the studio, working hard with Dupri on the next album. The problem was, between *Usher Live*, his movie projects, and preparing for the next disc, he'd had absolutely no down time in almost two years. Although he was young, wired on success and full of energy, he'd been stretching himself very thin. However strong he was, his nonstop schedule was taking a heavy toll on him.

Finally, in July 2000, he couldn't take it anymore. He was in the studio recording a track for his new album when, out of nowhere, he began to feel faint. Suddenly he collapsed. He was immediately rushed to the hospital, where he was found to be suffering from a combination of dehydration and exhaustion. What he needed was a little time off.

The trouble with taking time off was that there was a deadline looming for the early 2001 release of the new record. But his health was more important than the deadline, and everything was pushed back. What he urgently needed was a little rest and relaxation. And that was something his mother and manager, Jonnetta, made sure he got. No pressures, just a chance to come back down to earth, to sleep and be pampered by his mom for a little while. She did her best to look after him, and make sure no one tried to steer him wrong.

On top of his health issues, many of the songs from the upcoming album somehow found their way onto Napster, which at the time was considered a controversial (some said illegal) online file-sharing network. This is said to have been another reason to delay the release of the album. *MTV News* online reported Usher commenting, "After my music was released to Napster, I didn't think that was fair. . . . I didn't want that to be the way my record was remembered or the way I would present that to my fans."

In November 2000 the single "Pop Ya Collar" arrived, climbing into the Top 40, accompanied by a fifteen-track album called *All About U.* This album seemed to vanish as quickly as it arrived (it's now out of print, and copies are collectors' items). The album seemed to be LaFace Record's response to the illegal releases of his tracks on Napster. However, it was never intended to be the next Usher album.

All About U was somewhat of a phenomenon. Few people heard it, the album's single wasn't heavily promoted, and several of the cuts reappeared, in a slightly different form, a few months later on another album. Usher and everyone at the label were spending their time and energy on what would be the next proper release, which was still several months away. There was still plenty to be done in the studio, especially on the intricate final mixes of the tracks.

After a month off, with no talk of studios, discs, or anything related to business, Usher returned to work refreshed, reenergized, and raring to go. And there was still plenty of work to be done. As 2000 became 2001, Usher prepared himself for what he—and L.A. Reid—hoped would be his biggest year yet. The album, entitled *8701*, was set to arrive in August, and the single, "U Remind Me" would release in June.

While shooting the video for the single, he met Rozonda "Chilli" Thomas, one third of the vocal trio TLC. They were also from Atlanta, his homegirls, and they'd scored hit after hit for LaFace, making them labelmates with Usher. In fact, they'd first met when he signed with L.A. Reid, but he was just a teenager then, and she was seven years his senior—and a mother. Now things were different. He'd seen the world, experienced its ups and its downs, and become a man.

Chilli starred in the video for "U Remind Me," which went into immediate heavy rotation on MTV, boosting its success, and it was immediately obvious that there were sparks between the two of them. The seven years didn't matter anymore; this was true romance.

"I fell in love with her and her child," Usher admitted to *People Weekly Magazine*. And he did, big-time. Chilli's three-year-old son, Tron, was from a previous relationship. But Usher was just as taken with the boy as he was with her. And the feelings were mutual—Chilli fell for him, too.

It certainly seemed like a good thing. They were in the same business, and on the same level of success. They were both Atlantans, and they had a lot in common. Being in the same business, they both understood the pressures of fame and being on the road.

This relationship was the first time Usher had ever been seriously in love, which was both scary and exhilarating. Being in love as an adult, especially one with such a demanding career, was quite different from his teenage crushes. There was also a lot of responsibility that went along with being involved with someone who had a young son. But he was more than willing to take on all of that.

chapter five

That children were important to Usher was obvious to see from his charity work. He'd been involved with the Make-A-Wish Foundation, and had started his own charity, called the New Look Foundation, to offer a hand to less fortunate kids. He knew how lucky he'd been in his own life, not just because of the material success that had come his way, but in having a stable household to grow up in and a mother who was loving and responsible. As he noted in an article for insidecx.com, "someone has to look out for and protect our kids, and I feel blessed to be a blessing to someone else."

He happily participated in charitable events whenever he could, and donated some of his clothing and shoes—he reportedly owned 1,000 pairs—to various charities. His focus, understandably, was on kids in the Atlanta area, but his charitable deeds extended far beyond that.

By July 2001 Usher was all over the charts with "U Remind Me," which was rocketing up to the top position. And the album *8701* (the enigmatic title was supposedly a reference to his artistic growth between 1987, when he'd first started singing in church, and 2001) wasn't even due for another month. When it hit the stores, it flew off the shelves and immediately climbed straight to the top of the album charts in Canada. At home, however, it didn't sell as fast as its predecessor. Why that happened was a good question, especially because "U Remind Me" had done so well, and the follow-up, "U Got It Bad" was doing even better, spending an incredible ten weeks on top of the singles charts. But *8701* took off slowly. It took almost three months to sell its first million copies. By the end of the year it was at two million, and in January 2002 it was at three million—but still nowhere near the stunning seven million that *My Way* had managed.

This was both a surprise and a shock to Usher and Reid. They'd planned this very carefully. The album *8701* wasn't a radical departure from what had sold so well, although it did stretch Usher's limits a bit more. The ballads were stronger and deeper, and the dance songs were funkier. It was by far his strongest work to date, showing his growth (after all, four years had gone by since his last studio recording, not counting the half-release of *All About U*), which, given his age, had been rapid. There was a maturity, a rich soulfulness about his voice that made him stand apart from so many of the other young R&B singers. *Rolling Stone* awarded it three stars, saying "Usher's vocals are impressively adaptable," while *Vibe* said it contained "a steady supply of bump'n'grind promises to the ladies." The BBC said he was "fast becoming one of the hottest, multifaceted talents in the U.S.," with an "expert delivery" that was "full of soul and in control!"

Several producers worked on the album, apart from Usher himself (who'd also shown himself to be gifted in that field and subsequently began his own production company), including P. Diddy (formerly Puff Daddy), Babyface, the rising stars the Neptunes, and of course Jermaine Dupri and L.A. Reid. The result was an album that showed that Usher had come into his own and was now an R&B singer of real stature. He was versatile, easily able to handle both the slower, more emotional material as well as the faster-paced dance music. His range was greater, and with a few more years on him, as he was now the ripe old age of twenty-three, he'd become an important influence in both the R&B and pop music genres. With both "U Remind Me" and "U Got It Bad" topping the charts, he ended 2001 as the number twelve–ranked Singles Artist of the Year.

Though three-times platinum was only dim when measured against his last album's figures, Usher felt disappointed and put pressure on himself to do better. He wanted to be the best. As he told *The Dallas Morning News* decisively, "If you don't believe in yourself, nobody will." He believed he could well be the very best. That was his desire, to excel at everything he attempted, whether it was singing, producing, or acting.

In February 2002 Usher walked away with his first GRAMMY for Best Male R&B Vocal Performance, for "U Remind Me." It was a major moment, vindication of the path he'd taken, and a real sign of how far he'd come. This was a vote of confidence from his peers in the Recording Academy. *My Way* had sold brilliantly, and although *8701* did not reach the same sales heights, he was receiving artistic, as well as commercial, praise for his maturity and artistic growth.

His luck continued the following month, as 2002 seemed set to be Usher's year. In March the next single, "U Don't Have to Call," cracked the charts, and soon after, he won a Soul Train Music Award for Best Male R&B/Soul Album for *8701*. By April he was on the charts once again, although this time it wasn't under his own name. His one-time producer and mentor P. Diddy had asked Usher to be guest vocalist (along with Loon) on "I Need A Girl (Part One)," which was included on the album *The Saga Continues.* . . . It had been released as a single, making it to the top of several charts. He even picked up a Nickelodeon

Kids' Choice Award for Favorite Male Singer.

In May he was on the road, headlining with Faith Evans (who'd sung backup on *My Way* and was now a famous R&B artist), rapper Nas, and Mr. Cheeks on the Evolution 8701 World Tour. It was the longest tour he'd undertaken. They did take some short breaks, of course; it would have been impossible to keep up the pace otherwise. While it's difficult for any artist to be on the road for a long period of time, living in hotel rooms and out of suitcases, longing for the familiar comforts of home, it did have its compensations. Each show was a buzz, with screaming fans and sold-out venues all over the world. Contactmusic.com reported Usher saying "I feel the love from my fans now more than ever. Their responses are like instant gratification. It's like after all these years my hard work is paying off and my dreams are being answered. It's definitely a wonderful feeling."

He was in excellent shape, happy to flaunt

his washboard abs, which he'd achieved by a combination of weightlifting and swimming. What he certainly didn't realize at the time was that they'd become one of his trademarks, as readily identifiable as his face or his warm, soulful voice. While he was busy hitting the high spots around the globe, flashing his abs, and showing off his new dance moves, in May, "U Don't Have to Call" soared straight into the top ten, and in July, "Can U Help Me" hit the R&B charts and *8701* went four-times platinum.

In August, during one of his tour breaks, he attended the Teen Choice Awards and accepted two of them, one for Choice R&B/Hip-Hop Artist and one for Choice Love Song. He also won three Billboard Music Awards and was nominated for three MTV Video Music Awards. In September he was ranked number forty-seven in a list of the "100 Sexiest Artists" by MTV's sister station, VH1.

The media was all over him with

requests for interviews and most especially photo shoots—every cameraman, it seemed, wanted to capture those abs. Usher took full advantage of people's desire to see him. He even squeezed in time for a guest slot acting on the NBC drama series *American Dreams*, set in 1960s Philadelphia against the backdrop of social change that marked that decade.

The big thing looming on the horizon, however, was Usher's first DVD. *Live— Evolution 8701* was taken from the summer's tour. With fourteen songs plus a host of special features, it showcased his talents on stage, a reminder that he not only sang wonderfully, but he danced like a pop star, flowing easily and smoothly from one move to the next. All the hits were there, from "You Make Me Wanna . . ." onward, in addition to a short biographical video, clips of him rehearsing "U Don't Have to Call" with singers and dancers, a photo gallery, and discography.

It was more than a companion piece to *Usher Live*, which was only three years old. It was a way of capturing how much he'd grown as an artist. Comparing the two, it was immediately apparent that not only did the new Usher move with more grace and skill—the result of some imaginative choreography and an excellent natural ability—but he also sang with more confidence. He was more secure, not only in his position, but also in who he was.

Fan responses to the DVD commented on the dancing as much as the singing (especially on him pulling a girl from the audience and dancing with her), but that was no big surprise. For any act aiming at the mainstream pop market, dancing had become an integral part of the presentation, whether in a video or onstage. And Usher's fast feet and imaginative choreography were unmatched by most of the current pop stars. His fans were so impressed they began calling him Mr. Entertainment—for he was the guy who could do everything, sing, dance, and act, all while making it seem quite effortless. Only Usher and those closest to him knew how much hard work was involved in appearing so easy and relaxed.

He even took on "What's Going On," the signature tune of the late soul great Marvin Gaye. A complex, brooding piece about the state of the world that was as relevant in 2002 as when it was first released in 1971, it took soul to an entirely new level of complexity and feeling. Usher explored the depths of the song, losing himself in it and finding its emotional center. Notably, this time around, that was the only cover song; he'd moved past the need for the medleys that had helped fill out his last concert VHS.

Though his gestures on stage had to be extreme and exaggerated, away from the spotlight Usher tended to lead a very private life. Most of the time he was busy working on various projects. But everyone needs a break, and once the DVD had been released in a storm of press, Usher finally had the time to catch his breath for a few weeks.

He remained very private about his relationship with Chilli, and in an interview with *LAUNCH*, the online publication, he commented only that he was "in and out of a relationship" while recording *8701*. But in the world of show business, where everything was seen through a zoom lens, it was better for him to keep his love life out of the public eye. He and Chilli were still together, although it hadn't been easy, juggling their demanding careers and romance. In her case, too, she had to put her son first. It wasn't easy for either of them, and for weeks at a time, their contact was limited.

That year Chilli was also dealing with a tragedy, as a member of TLC and close friend, Lisa "Left Eye" Lopes, was killed in a car wreck in Honduras. Chilli and Tionne "T-Boz" Watkins, the third member of the group, had vowed to complete the album they'd been working on as a group when Lopes was killed, and they did. They released *3D* in September and received excellent reviews. The songs were a way of dealing with their grief, but Chilli had to come to terms with not only the loss of her friend, but also the end of her TLC career. With the tour and the demands of supporting a new album (which she was doing, too), it was hard for Usher and Chilli to spend a lot of time together.

February is often the most important month of the year for musicians, as that is when the GRAMMYs take place. Having scored once in February 2002, he was eager to repeat the feat. And he did. Once again he took home the GRAMMY for Best Male R&B Vocal Performance, for "U Don't Have to Call." It made the perfect end to what had proved to be his best year yet. Now *everyone* knew who Usher was.

chapter six

once he was back home, he had time to relax and enjoy being surrounded by people who mattered to him. He was free to indulge in his favorite seafood and soul food, and free to be spoiled by his mother, who would come over to cook his favorite comfort dinner of spaghetti. When *My Way* had sold so well, one of the first things he'd done was buy her the car she'd always wanted, a Mercedes. They always remained close, and even at this point in

Usher's stardom she remained his manager. With no father around, his mother and his brother had been the ones there for him, and Usher never forgot that.

It was almost impossible for Usher to relax for too long, however. Though he was still riding the wave of success that followed *8701*, the hit singles, and the tour's success, it was already time to begin thinking about the next record, although it wouldn't emerge for more than a year. This next disc was scheduled to be the big one, the album that would establish beyond any doubt that Usher was the top R&B singer in the world. He'd paid his dues, he'd established his success, and now he wanted to move so far ahead of the pack that no one could catch him.

He was also concerned about the direction R&B was taking, and wasn't afraid to say so. The music in general had gradually moved away from its roots, classic artists like Marvin Gaye, Smokey Robinson, and Stevie

Wonder, who'd helped define the genre in the 1960s. Even more recent acts like Prince and Michael Jackson had been a part of that continuum, and even they'd been left behind by the changes in the music.

Usher wanted to keep the old-school flag flying. As he commented on *MTV News* online, his goal was "just to hope-fully restore and continue to educate young people about R&B and what it really is." And what exactly was R&B to Usher? It was about a groove, and it was about emotion, the notion that the artists were spilling their hearts out in their songs. Much of that feeling seemed to have vanished from the scene, and so many people were unfamiliar with the older artists that they accepted the new R&B without reservation. With this new album, he intended to tighten that con-nection to the past, mostly through his lyrics. The groove was always important, and always would be, but he was determined that this new record would stand out lyrically from the ones he'd released before. "I've got a lot to say," he told MTV, adding that the record would be "a lot more personal than the last." Even more than *8701*, the new album would bring together both sides of his musical personality, with storming dance cuts and aching ballads. Having the concept was one thing. But translating that into an album of finished songs was a different matter. It was going to take more time and effort than he'd ever put in before. That was one reason for the lengthy break from touring and appearing in the public eye.

By this point in time he could afford his own studio, which at least simplified working. It was a place he could go whenever he felt inspired or when he wanted to try new things to see how they would work. But the real work would be done with outside producers. Usher himself, however, would be involved in every aspect and stage of the recording. This was his album, and he was determined to manage every detail to be sure it came out exactly as he wanted.

On top of preparing to record, he had other demands on his time. Those washboard abs didn't tighten by just lazing around. Along with meetings and studio time, he had workouts and dance rehearsals, often up to six or eight hours a day. And at night it wasn't unusual to find him out clubbing, enjoying himself and dancing some more.

It was a strenuous schedule, but he had the energy to cope with it. What was proving to be more difficult was his relationship with Chilli. They'd undergone a brief, mutual separation in the spring, only to come back together more powerfully than ever at the start of the summer. Chilli and her son, Tron, moved into Usher's mansion in Atlanta while her own house, which was also in Atlanta, was being refurbished. But being so close all the time put a strain on their romance. At the time it seemed to Usher that Chilli was looking to marry, to stay in Atlanta and settle down. He, however, was more restless. He was considering moving to New York or Los Angeles, and he wanted her to support that decision. But that was something she couldn't give; those were not the cities she wanted to live and raise a child in. She was older than he was, with the weight of responsibility for her son.

After a few months back together, they both decided that it simply wasn't going to work out—there were too many differences in what they wanted. The only answer was to go their separate ways, and as Usher told *People Weekly Magazine,* "I take responsibility for choosing another direction." It wasn't an easy decision for either of them. They'd been together for over two years, and they cared for each other deeply. On the outside Usher seemed to show no emotion about the breakup, but as people close to him said, inside he was hurting.

His breakup with Chilli, and relationships in general, were weighing heavily on his mind as he was writing and recording his slower ballads, but so, too, was the popular club music called crunk that played all over Atlanta. It had been big in the South for years, with its big, booty-shaking bass and rowdy, party atmosphere. Crunk had influenced the music of many Atlantan hip-hoppers such as OutKast and Ludacris, and their music in turn helped bring the style to a national level. As someone who loved to dance and go clubbing, Usher knew the crunk style well and decided to bring it into his new disc. The time was right, and if he could find the perfect song, it would fit in well, as long as he didn't lose the soul of R&B that would be the album's unifying thread.

There was even talk of a duet between Usher and Justin Timberlake. The former 'N Sync singer had forged a stratospheric solo career, and he had accomplished some very credible solo work that made him a teen idol in his own right. Justin and Usher were two of the biggest figures in music, and a track featuring the pair of them would have been a huge hit and a big seller. That would have been especially true if, as rumored, they teamed up with hot young producer Pharrell Williams. However, the project never went beyond the stage of preliminary discussions. Usher had talked to a few producers about the idea, and the two artists' managers had chatted. For the time being, however, it remained an idea and nothing more.

In his previous records Usher felt that he'd been almost like an actor playing different parts, inhabiting feelings that weren't really his. He'd managed it superbly and convincingly, of course—that was the art of the singer. And he'd done it in a way that had sold millions upon millions of albums and singles worldwide—a total of 24 million globally.

This time around he was a little older and felt the need to dig deeper into himself. "With every album, I try to better myself," he explained on his official Web site, usherworld.com. And while he admitted that he'd held something back emotionally before, he remarked, "This time, I decided to shake my fears and allow my personality to come through."

It was an audacious move, one that would leave him exposed and vulnerable if he followed through on what he promised. It also meant that lyrically he'd be making the kind of R&B record that hadn't been around since the 1970s, when singers and songwriters weren't afraid to wear their hearts on their sleeves and show their true emotions. But there was a fine line between confessions and self-pity. Usher and his producers were well aware of that. Given their track record together, it was assumed that Jermaine Dupri would be involved. He understood Usher and had watched him grow from a young man into a singer of international stature (although Dupri himself wasn't much older than Usher). But this was an album that would involve plenty of people, including some fresh blood: Jimmy Jam and Terry Lewis, who had worked with almost everyone in their lengthy careers and were still on top of the game; and Vidal and Dre (actually Vidal Davis and Andre Harris), who were up-and-coming, having worked on *The Diary of Alicia Keys*, as well as with Michael Jackson and Mariah Carey. Brian Michael Cox was also on board, cowriting a couple of songs. Producer-turned-artist Robin Thicke and Lil Jon, the self-proclaimed king of crunk whose dance music had been shaking club sound systems all over the Dirty South, were also involved.

Naturally Usher would have a hand in writing some of the material. On a record so personal, how could he not? But he was also willing to pick songs that captured the emotions he was looking for. This was a CD that would go beyond the image to the real man; it would reach deep inside and bare all—his responsibilities, anxieties, and, yes, even his failures.

One thing was true, he had a lot to live up to. Although *8701* hadn't broken sales records, it had taken Usher, the artist, to new heights. On the strength of his string of hit singles he'd virtually become a household name. Girls loved his voice, his looks, and that trademark six-pack. He was determined that this disc would be a major leap for him, remarking, "I'm really excited about this new project and I'm in a good place," the *Financial Times* reported. He needed to express the feelings he'd been bottling up for so long, and believed that doing so would help take his music to a new level. He was aiming to achieve the depth that the great singers and writers such as Smokey and Marvin Gaye had managed in their work. This time around Usher wanted to be taken seriously, as well as sell millions of albums. It was a great ambition, but one that wouldn't be easy to pull off. Yet if he didn't set ambitious goals for himself and continue to grow, he'd lose the respect of his fans and his peers—and eventually he'd lose respect for himself. He couldn't stick to formulas—that wasn't the ticket for him to move forward in life.

Usher was staking a lot on this album's release. It could make or break him, but he was willing to take that risk. He believed in what he was doing, and so did Jonnetta and his new label. Things had changed at LaFace: L.A. Reid had left to head up Arista, one of the major labels in the country, and Usher had migrated with him. With the change came an added pressure to sell more copies, especially in the business climate of consolidation and downsizing. Usher was in no danger of being dropped, but the expectations for the disc were high, perhaps higher than he would have wanted them to be. But he knew he could deliver.

He'd remained largely out of the public

eye throughout most of 2003, which suited him perfectly. When he returned to the limelight, it would be with a bang that would have everyone taking notice. The label had already decided that "Yeah!"—the track he'd recorded with Lil Jon and well-known local rapper Ludacris—would make the perfect first single. There was little disagreement. It had everything a single needed, with great beats, one of the catchiest synthesizer hooks in twenty years, and the mix of Usher's voice, which sounded richer than ever, and Ludacris's rap styles. It was a natural hit, all the executives agreed.

Usher celebrates the music of Earth, Wind & Fire at the 2004 Grammy Jam Fest to help raise funds for charity.

Usher talks with DJ Johnny Vaughn on Capital Radio in London.

Usher poses with Destiny's Child backstage at the
2004 Radio Music Awards.

Usher and Alicia Keys shoot the video for "My Boo" in New York City's Times Square.

© 2004 Getty Images

Usher signs copies of *Confessions* at the Union Square Virgin Megastore in New York City.

© 2004 Getty Images

Usher in the pressroom after the 2004 Billboard Music Awards.

Usher and Alicia Keys perform in London for BBC Television.

© 2004 Getty Images

Usher with Andre 3000 at the 2004 MTV Europe Music Awards.

© 2004 Getty Images

Usher and the Godfather of Soul, James Brown, performing at the 47th GRAMMY Awards®.

Usher poses with big-time hip-hop industry players, producer Jermaine Dupri and megastar Janet Jackson.

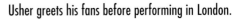

Usher greets his fans before performing in London.

Usher walks the red carpet in style at the 2004 MTV Video Music Awards.

chapter seven

As soon as "Yeah!" was released to radio, it spread over the airwaves like wild-fire. What Usher termed his "crunk'n'b" song was irresistible. No sooner was it in the stores than it appeared in the Top 40. The executives were right: "Yeah!" was the perfect single and a huge hit.

By February 2004 "Yeah!" was the top song in the country, seemingly glued to the top of the charts. But it almost didn't happen at all, as it turned out. When Usher first recorded the vocal over the track producer Lil Jon had concocted, everyone loved it. It had a great synth hook, deep, booming crunk bass, and fabulous beats. But what Lil Jon hadn't realized was the fact that he'd already shopped around his backing track and that Petey Pablo had used it for his record "Freek-A-Leek." Suddenly Lil Jon was sweating. Pablo's track had already been mixed and put onto vinyl. Pablo's label, Jive, had invested some serious money in it, and wasn't about to give it up for Usher, who recorded for the competition. As *Entertainment Weekly* reported, when L.A. Reid found out about the mix-up, he started "going crazy."

The only thing Lil Jon could do was head back into the studio and cook up something equally good. Now *that* was pressure. Amazingly, he managed it; some people would say he created something even better than the original. Certainly the public thought so, since "Yeah!" easily outsold "Freek-A-Leek."

However, the song also encountered

problems even before the mix-up. It had been written by Sean Garrett, a GRAMMY winner who'd penned songs for Destiny's Child, Jennifer Lopez, and Janet Jackson in the past. Although L.A. Reid liked the song, he wanted some of the lyrics reworked. But Garrett had a very strong vision for the song. He wanted to get Lil Jon and his crunk beats involved; Reid wasn't so sure. "I did at one point wonder if it was the right song for Usher," Reid admitted to the online publication, *Yahoo! News*. Once Reid agreed and the label approached Lil Jon, he didn't seem eager to sign on to the project. His manager initially said that he wasn't interested.

After it was completed, however, everyone was so convinced it would be a smash that they were anxious to have people hear it. And so, somehow, the disc found its way to radio stations well before its release date—which, Garrett admitted, was partly his doing. "Lil Jon and I leaked the record," he told *Yahoo! News*. Almost before anyone knew it, "Yeah!" was getting three thousand spins a week on the radio.

It seemed as if Atlanta had a lockdown on the singles charts. OutKast, who were also on Arista, had dominated the charts a few months before with "Hey Ya!" and now it was Usher's turn. His was a totally different sound, but it was equally catchy. "Yeah!" wasn't going to give up the top spot without a serious fight. Nothing else could even come close to it in sales, and soon it was topping an incredible *five* different *Billboard* charts, and showing no signs of moving.

It was a major success, as catchy as a cold, but far more satisfying. And it was a great omen for the album. It raised the anticipation, especially since it arrived two months before the disc, which would be titled *Confessions*, was due to release. "Yeah!" was an anthem for the radio and the dance floor, and vindicated all the belief that had been put in Usher. He could deliver exactly what everyone needed. Now everyone had to hope the album would do as well.

Usher tried to play down all the expectations, remarking to *Entertainment Weekly*, "You put a record together. You release it. It becomes successful or you go back in the studio and work on another album." But everyone was working on the assumption that *Confessions* would be a smash hit. It was set to appear in a glaring bash of publicity, and Usher was all over television, even performing live on the Internet in an AOL broadband concert. A European tour had been booked, and plans were already being solidified for a major U.S. tour in the coming summer. Over the space of three weeks, timed around the release of *Confessions*, Usher would hit *Good Morning America*, *Live with Regis and Kelly*, *Late Night with Conan O'Brien*, *The Tonight Show with Jay Leno*, *The Ellen DeGeneres Show*, *Jimmy Kimmel Live*, and *On-Air with Ryan Seacrest*. Now that was big. So the unbelievable popularity of

"Yeah!" came as a welcome relief to everyone—including Usher, whose reputation and artistic credibility were on the line. "Yeah!" was still the top single, its second month in the pole slot, and that stature would only be reinforced when the full publicity blitz began.

Like a player before a big game, Usher would psych himself up for the moment right before a new album would come out. He'd known disappointment before, with his debut *Usher* (now a full 10 years ago), and he'd known exhilaration and joy, which he'd experienced with *My Way*. He was used to the business's ups and downs, and he knew in his heart that this was the best work he'd ever done. He'd grown into the record, and made it a real reflection of who he was.

Meanwhile "Yeah!" made its way to the top of the U.K. charts, and as soon as *Confessions* was released in Britain and Canada it was an automatic number one in both countries. Now everything was falling into place. The album's single was a success in America and the album was a success in Britain and Canada, and Usher was excited for the big date at the end of March when the CD would be in American stores.

Finally the day of judgment arrived, and *Confessions* was released in the U.S. Everyone in Usher's camp was hopeful. But even the most ardent fan couldn't have predicted what would happen. According to the results from Soundscan, the company that tracks record sales, *Confessions* sold an unbelievable 1.1 million units in its first week on the shelves!

It was a record. Since the company began tracking figures for *Billboard* in 1991, no male R&B singer had even come close to the first week numbers that Usher's *Confessions* brought in. In its first week *Confessions* sold more than three times the number of albums that *8701* sold in its first week. Needless to say, *Confessions* went straight into the chart at number one.

It was the biggest debut week the Arista label had ever experienced in its thirty years of business, and a real vindication for Usher's dreams for the album. *Confessions* sales were also a reflection of the continuing popularity of "Yeah!," which was still dominating the singles charts. In order to ensure that "Yeah!" wasn't the only thing keeping the album alive, the label released a second single, "Burn," in April, which immediately crashed up the Top 40, and arrived in the top ten a month later.

Usher had always had faith that *Confessions* would be a landmark release for him, and he was grateful for the support Arista had given him. According to *Business Wire*, of Arista's unconditional support in helping his record get the acceptance that it deserved, Usher has said "there is no way for me to thank them enough."

Within a month of its release, *Confessions* had gone triple platinum, and by the end of

May it had sold four million copies. Four weeks after that, another million had been sold, collecting a total of seven million copies by the end of October. At the beginning of February 2005, almost a year after its release, it was still in the number seven spot on the *Billboard* album charts, with a staggering eight million copies sold, making it even more successful than 1997's *My Way*.

Usher ruled the charts, there was just no question about it. "Yeah!" was the top single for twelve weeks, until it was ousted by none other than his own second single, "Burn." What was it about Usher, and the songs on *Confessions*, that struck such a huge chord with America? His previous albums and singles had sold remarkably well, but never like this; it was as if everything had come together in one masterstroke.

And that, really, was what it was. He'd put together a perfectly balanced, expertly crafted album of songs, with lyrics that seemed to reveal the man behind the star. He had

worked so hard to get in touch with his emotions, to strip through the layers and get to
the heart of the words and of himself. In an
age of glossy productions, this was a great
feat, and both longtime fans and casual listeners obviously appreciated it. "Burn" kept a
hold on the top singles spot for more than six
weeks, and then "Confessions Part II," the
third single off the album, climbed to the
number two spot right behind it. Eventually
it took the top spot away from "Burn." It
seemed that the only person who was beating Usher in the charts was himself.

It wasn't completely unheard of for an
act to have three consecutive number one
singles. But it had only happened once
before, in 1964, when the Beatles achieved
the same incredible feat with "I Want to
Hold Your Hand," "She Loves You," and
"Can't Buy Me Love," giving them a total
of fourteen weeks at number one. Usher
had already surpassed that length. As if that
wasn't quite enough, "Confessions Part II"

was atop the Rhythmic Top 40, giving Usher his sixth number one on that chart, more than any artist had managed before.

He'd also accomplished one other not-so-small feat, and one that hadn't happened since he was born. "Yeah!," "Burn," and "Confessions Part II" had all been in the top ten at the same time, something only the Beatles and the BeeGees had managed to accomplish before him!

Believe it or not, this success was just the tip of the iceberg. Sales meant a lot, especially to recording companies. Since they were the ones who invested money in the artist, they wanted a solid return on their investment. But for Usher, record sales were just one weapon in his arsenal, albeit a very big one. A massive hit album would help bring people out to his concerts, where many of them would spend money on merchandise, which is always a big earner for musicians. The more concert tickets he sold, the wealthier he'd become.

He was busy, but not too busy to completely avoid a personal life. After the breakup with Chilli, he had kept a low personal profile, in part because he was spending so much time in the studio. But now Usher was back in the spotlight and out on the town, having the time of his life with beautiful new women on his arm. He was the hottest property in music, appearing on the cover of *Rolling Stone* and adding an appearance on *Saturday Night Live* to his extensive credits. He was undoubtedly a superstar, with his choice of women.

In June the annual BET Awards sent Usher home with two awards, the Male R&B Artist of the Year and the Viewers Choice Award, given for "Yeah!" It was the perfect reward for that single. You had to go a long way to find a more infectious song than "Yeah!" It had crossed over in the most effective way, a perfect mix of pop and R&B. The online publication *LAUNCH* called "Yeah!" "a genuine cyber funk masterpiece," and said that *Confessions* was "immaculate in fact; lean, smooth, slinky and, as an R&B album, expertly executed. It pulls all the right moves, in all the right places." Rollingstone.com gave it three stars. *Vibe* asserted that it "vaults him quite a ways from teeny-bopperdom into grown-man territory," praising the "sexy storytelling and surefire singles."

Sexy it certainly was. It wasn't so much a slow burn as a fiery sizzle throughout, with some startling lyrics. He raised eyebrows with his lyrics from "Confessions Part II," in which he whispered a secret that he was having a child with a girl he barely knew—although Usher would later indicate that wasn't true, just a line in a song. However, plenty of the pieces, such as "Follow Me," were autobiographical, Usher explains on his Web site usherworld.com, and tells fans that the song is "about a woman who treats me like a for-real, regular guy. . . ."

There was no shortage of sensual, slow jams. "Can U Handle It?" for example, is steamy, "the kind of song you put on . . . when the time is right!" he also explained on usherworld.com, "and yes, it could describe some real situations I've been in!" He was especially proud of "Superstar," for his singing, which contained a heartfelt depth that went beyond anything he'd managed before. Of the song, he has said on usherworld.com, "[I] wanted to show my growth vocally."

He firmly believed it was his best work to date. Amazon.com seemed to agree, calling it "Usher's coming of age record, bridging the gap from boy to man" in songs "that range from insinuating sultry R&B grooves to the decidedly crunky 'Yeah!'"

Something most reviewers commented on was the revelatory lyrics that exposed Usher's misdeeds, guilt, and needs. By the standards of modern R&B, it was almost outrageous. Usher was letting down his guard and inviting listeners into his head and heart, exposing all his secrets and desires. In that regard it was very old school, an album that went far under the skin. But even back in the day, few had done it in such a confessional manner as Usher achieved with this disc. The difficulty was sorting what was real from what was imagination and fantasy, and Usher left that to the listener.

The album did also contain some tributes to his personal heroes. "Do It to Me," for example, was very influenced by Prince in its ballad style, with Usher easily leaping into his high falsetto range. With *Confessions*, Usher established new territory for himself, away from artists like Justin Timberlake, who seemed to have taken over the pop end of the R&B market. This, as he'd intended, placed him in a direct line of R&B greats, from Donny Hathaway to Marvin Gaye, Michael Jackson, and Prince. Usher had taken the genre and reinvented it, as every good young artist should. He was aware of the roots of his music, and managed to stay true to them without being bound by old rules.

People responded to what Usher had to say, his admissions and claims, in a big way. Of course, it helped that they were disguised in such poetic terms, and with such expertly crafted music behind them, but it is rare to find a man willing to be so open, and openness is something his female fans valued. That's not to say that Usher was solely playing to the ladies, but they'd always been his biggest fans, and showing them his vulnerability, as well as his sensual side, made him not only a superstar, but a man that people could respect. Aside from "Yeah!" much of the album was an outlet for Usher's emotions. It was impossible to hear "Truth Hurts," the dynamic of an argument where you can almost hear a relationship falling apart, and not see Usher's human, vulnerable side. Everywhere, hearts were laid on the line. Sometimes they were broken, sometimes they were mended, sometimes sex was a Band-Aid, and sometimes desire overcame everything. But it was a disc that put the singer and the listener through the wringer. And that was its intention. The music was smooth, but the words were wrought with real life, love, and heartbreak.

chapter eight

The main thing people wanted to know about *Confessions* was just how autobiographical the songs really were. After all, Usher was dealing with plenty of deep, serious issues. To many listeners, it was a chronicle of his breakup with Chilli, although, as he told *Seventeen*, "I wasn't talking about my relationship with Chilli."

In truth, while the emotions in the songs were things he'd felt, the actual experiences described weren't his at all. He'd never been the guy in "Truth Hurts" who tries to hide his own guilt by becoming angry at his girl-friend, and there was no girl who was expecting his baby, as he'd written about in "Confessions Part II." He'd even written "Burn," about a relationship falling apart, while he and Chilli were still happily together. It was a case of having to separate the man from his art. With the breakup, however, it appeared that life was imitating art in Usher's case. Several months after *Confessions* came out, he'd even considered reconciling with Chilli. His house felt empty without her and Tron around. But finally, he admitted to *Rolling Stone*, he'd realized, "I think it's best that I don't call."

In early August 2004, Usher kicked off his Truth Tour in Virginia. It was going to be a long haul, running through October and covering most of the United States and Canada (he'd played dates in Europe during the previous spring). It was set to be one of the major tours of the year, simply because of Usher's massive popularity. And, of course, it demanded a lot of work and rehearsal. With the stage sets and the dancers, everything had to be choreographed and worked out in detail. Inevitably, there'd be plenty of dancing from Usher—he wasn't going to leave out something he did so well! The man Beyoncé Knowles once called "the Fred Astaire of our time," needed a chance to really show his stuff. The focus of the shows, of course, would be on the hits, and many of the songs from *Confessions.*

Usher promised his fans that each night would be a night to remember, and the shows would last almost two hours, with plenty of costume and set changes. With rising star Kanye West opening for him, it was an incredibly strong billing—almost as strong, in fact, as when Usher had opened for Janet Jackson.

Above all it gave Usher a chance to interact with his fans, the people who bought his music and put him in the superstar class. He didn't tour often, opting to spend much of his time in the studio, but as he remarked in *USA TODAY*, "going to the studio is good, but having that instant gratification and knowing how people feel about your performance is the best part."

When he was on the road there was no time to really think of relationships. He had to be focused on work, able to give his best night after night. While there were frequent days off between shows, a necessity for someone who depends on his voice, it was still a punishing schedule. Since the release of "Yeah!" he'd barely stopped working. But that was the cycle of things. After a full decade in the music business, he understood exactly how it worked.

Unlike many artists who were content to simply go in and sing, Usher had taken greater charge of his career, perhaps because his mother was his manager. She was always there to advise him, and keeping it within the family helped him keep things in perspective and reaffirm how important it was for him to be involved in his career, producing his own albums, and taking part in the decisions about his life. It was a good way to keep control and be in charge, and quite typical of "Mr. Entertainment." He knew he'd just scratched the surface of his potential. In addition to his own music, he'd decided to act on the idea of creating a record label, and formed US Records. He signed a couple of artists whose work was scheduled to release in 2005. And then there was also his movie career. Though he had set it aside for the last few years to devote himself more fully to music, there was still a great deal he wanted to do with that, and he was already making plans to star in several films, one of which would be a short film involving music.

At the start of August, however, that seemed a long way off. One of the first dates of the Truth Tour was in Toronto, where reviewer Jane Stevenson noted that even among all the hits and the dancing (Usher was backed up by a four-piece band and eight dancers), "nothing really matched his personal serenade to a woman he picked out of the audience and proceeded to seduce—complete with a bouquet of white roses—on a chaise lounge right in front of the besotted crowd."

He'd done that before, of course, but it was a prime moment of contact and connection with the fans, a chance for some lucky girl to get close to Usher. But that was one quiet moment in a show that was otherwise all singing, all dancing, and all energy. He was determined to give the fans value for the dollars they were dropping on tickets (demand for tickets in Toronto was so high, in fact, that Usher had to schedule a second date there in the fall). Usher was a professional. He knew what he needed to do to deliver, and that was the most important thing. Even traveling between cities, he was always attending to business. This would end up being one of the top tours of the entire year, grossing a staggering $29.1 million.

He was willing to make an additional stop when necessary, though, and one of them was in Miami, for the MTV Video Music Awards at the end of August. Usher had been nominated for Best Male Video, Best Dance Video, Video of the Year, Best R&B Video, and Best Choreography. Not only did he walk away with Best Male Video and Best Dance Video, but he also performed at the ceremony. Even though he had taken a break from his tour to attend, he couldn't turn down the chance to perform for his fans who, earlier that month, had awarded him Teen Choice Awards for Choice Album, Choice R&B Artist, Choice R&B Track and Choice Hook Up (given for "Yeah!").

He'd spent weeks on the top of the charts, broken all kinds of records, and was enjoying an incredible tour. How could he top any of that? With another hit record, of course. He'd recorded a duet with R&B diva Alicia Keys, called "My Boo," which was released as a single in September. It immediately flew into the Top 40. It would also appear on a new version of *Confessions* called *Confessions (Special Edition)*, which arrived in the stores in October. Adding a total of four tracks to the disc that was already quite long, he made it an even better value for the money. He included "My Boo," of course, along with "Red Light," "Seduction," and a remix of "Confessions Part II," given studio treatment by Shyne, Kanye West, and Twista.

The charts and Usher became inseparable companions for most of 2004. Fall was a whirlwind season for Usher. He picked up three World Music Awards for Best Male Artist, Best R&B Artist, and Best Pop Male Artist in September. "My Boo" continued to climb up the charts, and by October it was in the top ten. Not only was his tour progressing, selling out dates all over the country, but there were even more awards coming his way in October. He picked up two Source Hip-Hop Music Awards, one for Male R&B Artist of the Year, and one for Best R&B/Rap Collaboration of the Year for "Yeah!" Then "My Boo" topped the *Billboard*'s Hot 100 chart, Hot 100 Airplay chart, Hot R&B/Hip-Hop Airplay chart, Rhythmic Airplay chart, and Hot R&B/Hip-Hop Singles & Tracks chart.

Usher had made it back to number one—again. It was his fourth number one of the year, and meant that in the end he'd spend an unbelievable twenty-eight weeks in the top spot—that's seven months, more than half the year. He'd also made history as the first male lead to succeed himself in that top spot. Nobody, it seemed, could come close to matching his success. And with the new edition of his album in the stores, sales were soaring. To top that off,

Confessions went seven-times certified platinum, and singles "Yeah!" and "Burn" went certified gold.

As if all that wasn't quite enough, his mother and manager Jonnetta had been busy behind the scenes. Usher was no longer just a superstar, he was a brand. In a very unusual move, she'd negotiated with Mastercard for the issue of an Usher Raymond IV Debit Mastercard. Only one singer had had his likeness on a MasterCard before, and that had been one of music's great icons, Elvis Presley. Usher was following in some legendary footsteps.

Although it may have seemed like an odd move, there was certainly some logic to it. Usher had fans of all ages, not just teenagers. His R&B sound, with its strong acknowledgment of the past, reached across generations. And quite a few of those might want to show their allegiance to their hero by carrying an Usher MasterCard.

While still riding high with "My Boo,"

the American Music Awards occurred in November. By now the Truth Tour had ended, and Usher was hard at work on his short music film. But he made the time to go and perform at the ceremony, which seemed only fair, as he was up for five of the awards, including Artist of the Year. As it was, he had trouble getting off the stage that evening, since he found himself accepting four different plaques—Favorite Soul/R&B Male Artist, Favorite Soul/R&B Album, Favorite Pop/Rock Male Artist, and Favorite Pop/Rock Album.

As amazing as that evening must have been for Usher, it was simply a preview of what was to come at the Billboard Music Awards in early December, which became the single biggest night of Usher's career. Not only was he nominated in more categories than could be counted on two hands, he was also opening the show.

He made his appearance in fine style,

dropping from the ceiling to join a group of female dancers to perform "Bad Girl" in the kind of singing and dancing extravaganza that has rarely been seen in the last few years. The choreography was wonderfully inventive, and even though he was constantly in motion, Usher never missed a note, sliding up against guitarist Dave Navarro (from Jane's Addiction) who helped out on the song.

The whole night was a high. Keys took home seven awards, but in 2004 no one was going to outdo Usher. By the time the proceedings were over, he'd won awards for Artist of the Year, Billboard 200 Album of the Year, Billboard 200 Artist of the Year, Hot 100 Single of the Year, Hot 100 Artist of the Year, Hot 100 Airplay Single of the Year, R&B/Hip-Hop Album of the Year, R&B/Hip-Hop Album Artist of the Year, R&B/Hip-Hop Artist of the Year, Mainstream Top 40 Artist of the Year, and Mainstream Top 40 Single of the Year. Usher had won an unbelievable *eleven* trophies in a single evening!

It would be a year to remember for the rest of his life, although Usher hoped that soon he'd top it and do even better on his next album.

chapter nine

with the incredible success of 2004
under his belt, Usher was hard at work on a gift
for his fans to ring in 2005. He'd been crazily
busy with what he called a "minimovie,"
although it was really more of an extended
music video. Twenty minutes long and featuring a crew of guests that included P. Diddy,
Naomi Campbell, and Clifton Powell, *Rhythm
City Volume 1: Caught Up* contained a DVD
and a CD. The DVD featured five videos from
Confessions—"My Boo," "Yeah!," "Burn,"

"Confessions Part II," and "Caught Up," as well as behind-the-scenes footage. The CD featured three new tracks, including "Seduction," "Red Light," and "Take Your Hand."

It premiered on FOX's *New Year's Eve: Live from Times Square with Ryan Seacrest* (who also had a cameo role in the movie), and formed a major exclusive for the network. Having Usher's film was a way to guarantee a large audience.

Usher delivered something special to fans prior to the commercial DVD release of the minimovie. On February 21 his minimovie was given a screening at forty-four theaters nationwide, along with a live interview with Usher, conducted by Lionel Ritchie. Showing the minimovie in theaters two weeks ahead of the commercial release date for the DVD was Usher's way of saying thank you to those who'd supported him.

Why did Usher make it? It wasn't something he had to do. But it formed a way back into a different kind of filmmaking for him.

He'd already acted, and he was a veteran of music videos. But he'd never worked on developing a concept and taking charge of a movie before. He wanted to explore the nuances and possibilities of that. As he noted in *Teen People*, "Producer, director, writer . . . there are so many avenues."

It was an indication that Usher was seriously considering being on the other side of the camera in the future, although he still had many years ahead as a star. But it was typical of his logical, long-term approach of thinking ahead. More immediately, however, he was preparing to start a year dedicated to movies, which included a couple of starring roles.

He had become well known and famous enough that he was asked to be a presenter at the Golden Globe Awards in the middle of January, and took advantage of the invitation to make sure he hit *all* the after-show parties.

The year 2005 was starting out just as busily as 2004 had ended. Usher had helped

Ludacris and Lil Jon out on the track "Lovers and Friends," which crashed into the Top 40 in January, and climbed into the top ten later in the month. By the middle of the month he'd picked up a People's Choice Award for Favorite Male Singer. "My Boo" and "Burn" had gone certified platinum by the time January ended, and just to make sure he finished January in a warm climate, he jetted off to Cannes, in southern France, for the NRJ Awards, where he performed and also received the International Male Artist of the Year award.

In response to the album's overwhelming success and the artist's undeniable growth and talent, January landed Usher with an unbelievable *eight* GRAMMY nominations. The GRAMMYs are the most prestigious awards in the field of music, the equivalent of the Oscars for film and the Tonys for theater. He was up for Best Rap/Sung Collaboration for "Yeah!," Best Male R&B Vocal Performance, Best R&B Song for

"Burn" and "My Boo," ("Yeah!" was also nominated although Usher was not involved in writing this song), Best R&B Vocal Performance By a Duo or Group for "My Boo" with Alicia Keys, Best Contemporary R&B Album for *Confessions*, Record of the Year for "Yeah!," and the coveted Album of the Year for *Confessions*.

Usher, however, was philosophical about his chances. "I recognize that this hard work did not go unnoticed and if I do not win Album of the Year, which is the one I'm most interested in winning, then so be it," he told *Jet* magazine.

But it wasn't as simple as that. Though his words did not show it, he held back his deep desire to win. He'd had the chart success, and despite all the other awards he had won, winning those GRAMMY Awards would be the real reward.

Although the coveted Album of the Year went to the late great Ray Charles for *Genius Loves Company*, Usher did not walk away empty-handed by any means. *Confessions* won for Best Contemporary R&B Album, "My Boo" brought both Usher and Alicia Keys (who took home a total of four GRAMMYs) onstage to accept for Best R&B Performance by a Duo or Group with Vocals. And finally "Yeah!" got credit for being the biggest song of 2004, winning Best Rap/Sung Collaboration.

Usher certainly arrived looking the fashionable part, dressed in a white, jacketless suit, sporting a brown tie, two-tone spectator shoes, and of course, his sunglasses. He changed his costume for his onstage debut with the godfather of soul himself, the venerable James Brown. Their performance was phenomenal, and even though Usher didn't take home as many GRAMMYs as he'd hoped he would, one thing did cap off the evening: He went home having won something that no one else could have—the great honor of being named the "godson of soul," minted by the godfather himself.

The year 2005 continued to shine with nominations for four NAACP Image Awards, including Outstanding Male Artist, Outstanding Music Video (twice, for "Yeah!" and "My Boo"), Outstanding Song, and Outstanding Album, followed by the Soul Train Awards nominations, which included Best Male R&B/Soul Single, Best Group, Band, or Duo R&B/Soul Single, Best Male R&B/Soul Album, the Michael Jackson Award for Best R&B/Soul or Rap Music Video, and Best R&B/Soul or Rap Dance Cut.

So it was no surprise he was a winner at the Soul Train Awards, carrying off two of his own—for Best R&B/Soul Album (*Confessions*) and Best Male R&B/Soul Single ("Confessions Part II"), as well as sharing a third (Best R&B/Soul Single by a Duo or Group) with Alicia Keys for "My Boo," and another with Lil Jon and Ludacris for Best R&B/Soul or Rap Music Video for "Yeah!"

However, it wasn't as if he didn't have anything else to do. He was already rehearsing for his next project, which was going to take him back to acting. He'd landed a lead role in the movie *Dying for Dolly*, a Mafia romance, with Usher playing opposite veteran actor Chazz Palminteri.

"This is sort of my hiatus from music, and I wanted [this movie] to be a project that would be outside the box and not what you would normally expect," he explained on MTV. In the script Usher's character falls in love with Dolly (played by Emmanuelle Chriqui, who'd been in *On the Line* with former 'N Sync star Lance Bass), the daughter of a Mafia boss. Usher told MTV in an interview that it's "a story about love and the obstacles you'll go through in certain situations."

While it strayed from the subject matter of Usher's previous films, he was attracted to the script, and was looking forward to working with the director, Ron Underwood, who has made a number of films, including *City Slickers*. Usher's character, Darrell Williams, is set to be a producer and the head of a record label, as well as a DJ—but one thing he doesn't do (although Dolly tries to make him) is dance! He prepared for the role by working extensively with Underwood, taking plenty of notes, and coming in with an innate understanding of his character's hopes and dreams. Apart from that, Usher noted in his interview with MTV, "it was pretty easy in the sense of understanding the love story." But he was under no illusions about the amount of work he'd have to do. The filming was intense, and incredibly time-consuming and demanding; everything tied around a tight budget of time and money, involving long, long days on the set.

He admitted that he was looking for other films to make in 2005, too, and he'd previously mentioned the possibility of doing a biopic on Jackie Wilson, one of the very early soul legends from the 1950s and

1960s, a singer who Usher felt had never been given his proper acclaim. But Usher was looking at a couple of other names, too, including Sam Cooke and Marvin Gaye, both great, lauded soul singers. Which one ends up being made remains to be seen, but from Usher's level of interest, it seems almost a certainty that one of them will.

He has also been announced as the star of another film, *Step in the Name of Love*, tentatively scheduled for 2006. It is a dance musical about steppin', an urban swing dance that was popular in Chicago. Also set to star is Holly Davis-Carter, and Jonnetta Patton, Usher's mom and manager. Beyond that, no details have been released except that Usher intends to be active behind the camera as well as in front of it—not as the director, but as the movie's producer. Though it seems that Usher will take some time off from music to continue his acting, as always, he will stay true to his fans and continue to bring some music their way.

In March 2005, Usher's *One Night, One Star: Usher Live* remake of his Truth Tour aired on Showtime, a heavy-budget live show direct from Puerto Rico. An absolute indication of his superstar status, Showtime made many publicity arrangements to advertise his appearance. In addition to the concert itself, there was also backstage and behind-the-scenes footage. "You're going to see a lot of the songs that were made number one in 2004, as well as music from my earlier albums. And expect nothing but live . . . live, yes! vocal performances! You'll be entertained from the beginning until the end," he told teenmusic.com. Entertaining was key, and Usher had grasped that very firmly. The idea of being Mr. Entertainment rings more and more truthful for Usher, with careers on both sides of the movie camera, and both sides of the desk, as he kicks his record label into gear later in 2005. Show business has been his life since his early teens, and he's making sure it remains that way, exploring every possible avenue to find his own success in it.

He's certainly not afraid of hard work, throwing himself wholeheartedly into every project. But that kind of commitment is the only way to succeed. It's how he has made it this far. From the moment he decided he wanted to be a singer, he dedicated himself to that goal, convincing his mother, convincing everyone, and even managing to overcome the obstacle of losing—rising again after his first album had failed to become a success.

He's always believed in himself and his abilities and talent. Usher has shown a very smart business sense, although of course he could not have gained such an understanding without a good coach standing by, his manager and mother. They both understand that business is a vital part of music, and the more control an artist has over his own work, the better things will be for him in the long run. This is partly why Usher has taken to being the executive producer of his albums, why he's diversified into movie production, and why his mother negotiated having his own brand of debit MasterCard.

Singer, dancer, actor, businessman—they're all necessary facets before one can become a true, ultimate superstar and a true entertainer. But Usher would be nowhere without his dedication, hard work, ambition, drive to push through the struggles and the hardships, and the confidence to pick himself up when he falls and continue to pursue his dream.

As he commented in an interview on teenmusic.com, "My first album dictated my confidence because of everything that went into it and all of the adversity that I had to deal with. The second album, I had regained my voice. As a vocalist I began to try new things. Got my first hit record. The next album, I began to give you great stories and pay homage to the people who had come before me. *Confessions*, man, it was like here it is all or nothing. It's a process."

One can only imagine the heights that Usher Raymond IV will reach as he grows as an artist, an actor, a producer, and a person. Though his achievements and accolades are many, one can be sure that the world hasn't seen the last of Usher's talents, the end of his growth as an artist, or the peak of superstardom for the godson of soul.

acknowledgments

AS ALWAYS, I'm grateful to my agent, Madeleine Morel, without whom this book wouldn't have happened. Huge thanks to Orli Zuravicky at Simon & Schuster, my editor on this; it's a pleasure to work with you. The Seattle Public Library, as ever, proved to be the font of all knowledge (as well as plenty of great books). Pepper put up faithfully with my typing and researching, Aire listened to me rabbiting on and offered continual encouragement. Linda Hornberg supplied the copy of *Jet* and the roof. Graham Nickson supplied a son's love, which means the world to me. Thom Atkinson supplied the friendship, as he has for a long time now.

I'm grateful to the following articles for the information they supplied: Usher with Sway (MTV Interview); "Usher: Be Our Valentine," by Lynn Barker (Teen Music); "Usher: Yeah Baby," by Neil Drumming (*Entertainment Weekly*, December 31, 2004); "Usher Crowned the 'King of Pop' by *Billboard*"(PR Newswire, December 23, 2004); "Usher to Debut Mini–Movie" (UPI, December 26, 2004); "Usher Owns Top Two" by Fred Bronson (*Billboard*, June 26, 2004); "Usher's Smash 'Yeah!' Almost Made," by Eliott C. McLaughlin (AP, February 2, 2005); "Usher Sets All-Time 1st Week Soundscan Sales Record" (Business Wire, March 30, 2004); "The Story Behind the Hit," by Neil Drumming (*Entertainment*

Weekly, May 14, 2004); "Usher in a New Era," by Anne Marie Cruz (*People*, April 19, 2004); "Usher Souled Out" by Shaheem Reid (MTV News.com); "Usher Uncensored" (*Teen People*, May 2004); "Usher, When's the First Time U," by Jonathan Small (*Teen People*, May 2004); "From Usher with Love" (Europe Intelligence Wire, April 8, 2004); "Ushering in a More Mature Sound," by J. R. Reynolds (*LAUNCH*, November 7, 1997); Inside Cx feature, date, and author unknown; "All Lit Up," by Billy Johnson Jr. (*LAUNCH*, January 21, 2000); "Former Teen Star Usher Remains on Top at 25" (*Dallas Morning News*/Knight-Ridder/Tribune News Service, August 10, 2004); "The Real King of Hip-Hop," by Jeff Lorez (*LAUNCH*, July 27, 2001); "The Remix of Usher" (*Jet*, February 7, 2005); "25 Hottest Stars under 25" (*Teen People*, June/July 2004); "Usher," by Holly Eagleson (*Seventeen*, May 2004).